she minds her own business

WORKBOOK

KRYSTEL STACEY

Published and distributed by Merack Publishing.
Stacey, Krystel, 1986 - She Minds Her Own Business

ISBN: 978-1-949635-41-6

Printed in the United States of America

"She" is an entrepreneur who designed her life and loved every inch of it.

She was not worried about what "they" were doing or how they defined success.

She didn't listen to what they had to say because she wasn't doing it for "them."

She set her own standards and priorities.

She pursued her goals and lived life to its fullest potential.

She kept her head in the clouds and her feet on the ground.

She stayed focused on the *joie de vivre,* celebrating the joy of life with each and every tiny victory.

My hope is that by the end of this book,

"she" is **you.**

In the pages that follow, I will walk you through how I became this woman—and how you can become her too.

You were
made for

brilliance, darling.

Step into it.

- Krystel Stacey

#SheMindsHerOwnBusiness

cou·ture

/ko͞oˈto͝o(ə)r/

noun

the design and manufacture of fashionable
clothes to a client's specific requirements
and measurements.

fashionable made-to-measure clothes.

"Maria's couture gown was designed
specifically for her by a renowned designer."

#SheMindsHerOwnBusiness

CHAPTER

N⁰1

DESIGNING YOUR COUTURE LIFE & BUSINESS

I believe you have to start by working on your life to get to a place where you are ready to work on your business. The two spheres go hand in hand, and so often, your attention spent on one is the cause of your neglected attention to the other. My goal is to let you practice and get up to speed, so that you can work on both harmoniously.

1. What do you really, actually, truly want?

2. Does this align with the path you are on now?

3. What has been holding you back from living your life in the way you want?

"

"My life didn't please me, so I created my life."

COCO CHANEL

#SheMindsHerOwnBusiness

4. How would you do things differently if you got to start over?

5. What have you been expecting that might be unrealistic?

6. How are you going to get to your end game? List broad ideas... we are going to dive deeper in each chapter.

This last question is vital. If you have no idea how to answer it, give yourself a deadline (no longer than a month) and pause here. Take the time to deeply reflect and answer this question before moving on.

What 3 things can you change in your life right now, before continuing this process, that will make a mighty difference in your mindset? For instance, designating a place or time block in which you can devote your attention to this work will go a long way. Maybe it's cleaning your desk off, buying a new candle to make your space smell fresh, getting out your favorite pen to write with, or turning off your phone for an hour each day to work on this. It's your life; you know what you need to do!

1

2

3

NOW DO THOSE THINGS. Crossing them off the list will feel so good!

This is your
life, your one and only
precious life. It's time for
you to take control and

design a life,

you love.

———

Krystel Stacey

Social Challenge

We have included Social Challenges throughout the book as a way for you to act, present, and put out into the world what you are learning in an effective way. We designed these challenges to be at pivotal points in the book where we feel you should share with your audience (whether you have one follower a million).

These were created to help you express your goals, and to TAKE ACTION as you design a life and business you love. Too often we aren't sure where to start when it comes to sharing or how much to share so we are guiding you through step by step and have created challenges that we know will be inspiring to you and your following.

*"I found after **posting**, that many people are there ready to support me in my **dreams**. With this understanding, my fears become smaller and I became more **confident** in myself."*
– Tina Sullivan, entrepreneur & graphic designer

Take some time and write down choices you have made out of a sense of obligation.

1. What did you do because someone else told you to, because someone said that was the right choice, or because someone thought that was what you needed to do?

2. How did it make you feel? What did you learn from it then? What can you learn now?

"I believe that we are solely responsible for our choices, and we have to accept the consequences of every deed, word, and thought throughout our lifetime."

———

ELIZABETH
KÜBLER-ROSS

#SheMindsHerOwnBusiness

To get your life from point A to point B, you should start thinking more creatively about how you can move to where you want to be in five years. This can be a very broad brain-dump of ideas, but it's time to write them down. Remind yourself where you want your life to be in five years, and focus on a single part of it for this exercise.

1. Where are you now? (This is point A)

2. Where do you want to be? (This is point B)

3. What's the "traditional" path from point A to point B?

4. What is an out-of-the-box way to get from point A to point B? Take 10 minutes and list as many paths as you can think of.

5. Rank your ideas, including the traditional path, starting with 1 for your very best idea.

6. Now that you've listed your top ideas, take the top 3 and test them out. Meet with someone you trust, over social media or in person, and go over these top 3 ideas with them, to get feedback. Pursue each option until you get real feedback, not just a stamp of approval.

To get your business from point A to point B, perform the same exercise as in Session #3, above. Where do you want your business to be in 5 years? Now, in general terms, focus on a single part of that goal.

1. Where are you now? (This is point A)

2. Where do you want to be? (This is point B)

3. What's the "traditional" path from point A to point B?

4. What is an out-of-the-box way to get from point A to point B? Take 10 minutes and list as many paths as you can think of.

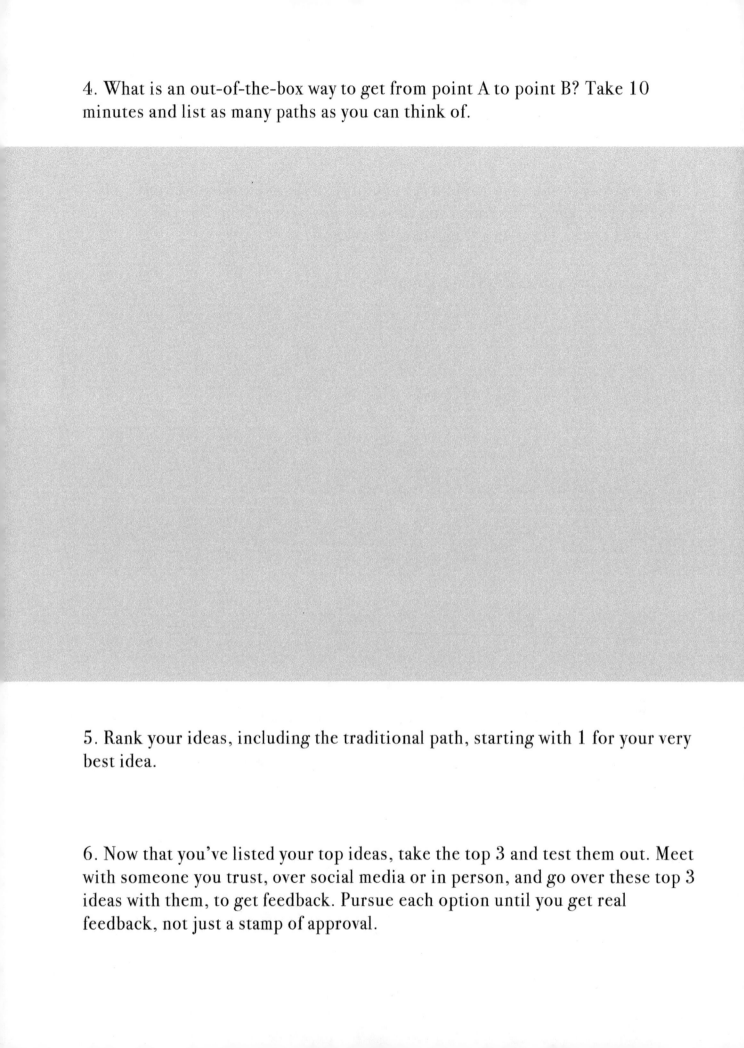

5. Rank your ideas, including the traditional path, starting with 1 for your very best idea.

6. Now that you've listed your top ideas, take the top 3 and test them out. Meet with someone you trust, over social media or in person, and go over these top 3 ideas with them, to get feedback. Pursue each option until you get real feedback, not just a stamp of approval.

own it own it ou

own it own it o

it own it

own it

it own it

Chapter 1 Review

After reading Chapter 1 in She Minds Her Own Business, survey yourself. Here are some prompts to get you started in designing your dream life and loving every inch of it.

1. What do you currently LOVE about your life?

2. What do you currently wish you could change about your life?

3. What do you currently LOVE about your business?

4. What do you currently wish you could change about your business?

5. What does your daily life look like right now?

6. Five years from now, what does your dream life look like?

7. Five years from now, what does your dream business look like?

8. What do you currently wish you could change about your business?

9. What does your daily life look like right now?

10. Five years from now, what does your dream life look like?

11. Five years from now, what does your dream business look like?

> In order to be irreplaceable, one must always be **different.**
>
> —Coco Chanel

#SheMindsHerOwnBusiness

12. Who in your life intimidates you, makes you feel small, or sucks energy out of you? In other words, with whom should you be spending less time?

13. Who in your life inspires you and makes you want to be a better person? How can you spend more time with them?

14. Who in your industry intimidates you? How can you turn around this intimidation?

15. Who in your industry inspires you? How can you let them know you admire them?

You are off to a great start. GET IT, GIRL!

Social Challenge

FOR YOUR INSTAGRAM AND FACEBOOK STORIES

Share that you are reading a new book... "She Minds Her Own Business" and that you are going to OWN IT (your business, your life, and this workbook). Share your greatest takeaway from this first chapter and how you are going to live differently, how it's changed your thought process, or helped you see things from a new perspective.

*Add the hashtag #SheMindsHerOwnBusiness and tag @krystelstacey for repost.

CHAPTER

2

PASSION, PURPOSE & SUCCESS

suc·cess
\sək-ˈses
noun
1. outcome, result
2. degree or measure of succeeding
3. favorable or desired outcome
4. the attainment of wealth, favor, or eminence
5. one that succeeds

— Merriam-Webster Dictionary

#SheMindsHerOwnBusiness

Let's define your own personal idea of success: what success looks like to you. Its meaning is different for every person on this planet, which can be confusing —so I want you to get really clear about what success is to you.

I'll walk you through a series of questions to help you decide what your most successful, beautiful, and radiant self looks like. Then we can take a step back and define it for you.

To find your purpose, let's start with your passions:

1. What are you passionate about now?

2. What have you been passionate about in the past?

3. What makes you excited to get up every day?

4. What do you enjoy doing most in your current job?

5. What do you dread doing?

6. When do you feel most alive?

7. When do you feel like your best self?

"

**"When
you are living in your
purpose and you are defining
your own success, this is when
you have made it!"**

KRYSTEL STACEY

8. Who makes you feel like your best self?

9. What makes you unique?

10. What makes you feel accomplished?

11. What are you currently unsure about?

12. What do you know with all of your heart?

13. What do you want for your future?

14. Looking holistically at your lists from the last two pages, what stands out as a common thread? Even if you aren't sure if that is your purpose, begin writing what it could be.

Write down every possibility that comes to mind.

Did I live?

Did I love?

Did I matter?

–

Brendon Burchard

#SheMindsHerOwnBusiness

Social Challenge

FOR YOUR INSTAGRAM AND FACEBOOK STORIES

If there is a part of the book you are struggling with, or if you want to gain clarity about yourself - asking friends and family is a great way to do it and create engagement on your Instagram.

Also posting something such as - I am working on defining my purpose, what I already know about myself is ... (be confident about what you already know and who you are.) It would help if you would post one word that describes me (use the question feature).

Or have them take a poll if you are trying to narrow it down between a couple of different words you can use to define your purpose. Of course it can be two or three words, but this helps you and them to see you for who you really are—you beautiful person, you!

DO NOT LET THEM DEFINE YOU but this is one fun way you can interact with your audience, gain insight, and share a bit about who you are with them.

*Add the hashtag #SheMindsHerOwnBusiness and tag @krystelstacey for repost.

Now, which ONE out of these possibilities stands out most to you? Which thing could you do forever and never get tired of? Many of your passions have this thing in common. Which one or two make you feel most FULFILLED? Is there a way to combine more than one?

THAT IS YOUR PURPOSE!

My purpose is to:

Seriously, for now—keep
your head in the clouds.

dream girl, dream!

Write it all down.

———

Krystel Stacey

Social Challenge

LET'S GROW YOUR FOLLOWING ON INSTAGRAM AND FACEBOOK

I want you to make a new post on Instagram (picture of you or something that inspires you) re-introducing yourself on your Instagram with your PURPOSE clearly written out. You can also list a few of your passions if you want to make it a "get to know me post" and some of your struggles. People on Instagram and social media are longing for authenticity so if you can be real, clear, and authentic with them, the post will be a WIN!

*Add the hashtag #SheMindsHerOwnBusiness and tag @krystelstacey for repost.

Write down who you currently are and where you are in your life...

1. Who are you?

2. Where are you?

3. What are you doing for work?

4. What are you doing for fun?

5. Who are you with?

6. Who are your friends?

7. What does your day-to-day look like?

8. Where do you live?

9. What does your house feel like?

10. Where do you spend your time?

NOW...

Imagine the very best version of yourself 5 years from now (if you accomplished all of the goals you are about to set)...

1. Who are you?

2. Where are you?

3. What are you doing for work?

4. What are you doing for fun?

5. Who are you with?

6. Who are your friends?

7. What does your day-to-day look like?

8. Where do you live?

9. What does your house feel like?

10. Where do you spend your time?

Are you dreaming big? Can you dream bigger?
Of course you can! Go back and fill in more details.

Success:
the accomplishment of an aim or purpose

Purpose:
the reason for which something is done or created or for which something exists

Passion:
a strong feeling of enthusiasm or excitement for something or about doing something

#SheMindsHerOwnBusiness

Look at your responses above.

1. What does this "future most successful self" have that you currently don't?

2. How are you going to get it?

3. What do you need to get to that point?

4. How would the most successful version of you describe success?

Social Challenge

FOR YOUR INSTAGRAM AND FACEBOOK STORIES

I think getting real on social media (AND BEING CONFIDENT ABOUT WHO YOU ARE AND WHERE YOU ARE GOING) is important and will make all the difference in who you are attracting. Also telling them who you are, the words that define you, and your purpose will give them a better understanding, letting them know that it's deeper than the product or service you are selling, there is meaningful purpose.

*Add the hashtag #SheMindsHerOwnBusiness and tag @krystelstacey for repost.

Okay, now that you know your purpose, you can fully define your own success:

1. I feel successful when:

2. When I wake up in the morning as my most successful self,

I see:

I smell:

I hear:

I feel:

I
will make everything
around me
beautiful,
that will be my life.

———

Elsie de Wolf

3. These are the people with whom I have surrounded myself:

4. This is how often I work:

5. I will be fulfilling my purpose by:

6. My relationship with money looks like:

Now, write out what your most successful self is like, as if "she" already exists. What would make you say, "I can't believe this is my life?" Really put yourself in her shoes. Write out an entire specific day.

Now look back at that last page. The things you listed are all important, but isolate the parts that are MOST important to you to DEFINE SUCCESS.

Write your definition of **success** here:

Then write it everywhere: on your mirror, in your car, as your phone's lock screen—as a reminder to yourself of what success looks like to you.

"I will *inspire* those around me to become better. To remember who they were before others broke them down. Reminding myself and them daily to be the people they were made to be. Bringing *vision* and providing *clarity*.

I will *create* every day and dream big. I will live out the life I have *imagined*. I will bring *joy* to those around me and be a *light* to those who know me. I will live a life of *purpose*, not just a life of what comes my way.

———

KRYSTEL STACEY

#SheMindsHerOwnBusiness

Social Challenge

LET'S GROW YOUR FOLLOWING ON INSTAGRAM AND FACEBOOK

Create a post with a photo that inspires you and share what success is to you. "You do you" and share how you would normally share things that inspire you. Maybe encourage your followers to define their success, or spend time today envisioning success for themselves?

*Add the hashtag #SheMindsHerOwnBusiness to join our community and tag @krystelstacey for repost.

Remember:

"you do you!"

- Krystel Stacey

#SheMindsHerOwnBusiness

3.

VALUES

AND

PRIORITIES

 Key Areas of *Joie de Vivre*

SURROUNDINGS.

RECREATION & RELAXATION.

PERSONAL GROWTH.

SPIRITUALITY & FAITH.

PURPOSE & CAREER.

FINANCES.

FRIENDS & FAMILY RELATIONSHIPS.

ROMANTIC RELATIONSHIP(S).

FITNESS & PHYSICAL HEALTH.

EMOTIONAL HEALTH.

GIVING.

EXPLORE.

#SheMindsHerOwnBusiness

1. Take some time and write down everything you value.

2. What values do you believe in holding above all else?

3. What really tugs on your heartstrings that may be unique to you?

These are your personal values, things that matter most to you!

"

What's holding you back?

KRYSTEL STACEY

#SheMindsHerOwnBusiness

How to rank the key areas of your life:

STEP 1: A DEEP DIVE

Rate your level of fulfillment with each area of your life below. Use a scale of 1 to10, with 1 being extremely dissatisfied/very unfulfilled and 10 being extremely satisfied and fulfilled. Each area will be rated individually, so each one could have the same rating. I include a description of each section, but remember that fulfillment and happiness in a particular area should be defined solely by you.

12 Key Areas of *Joie de Vivre*

circle your level of fulfillment with each area of your life.

not very   *very*

SURROUNDINGS

This is where you spend most of your day. It includes your environment, the town you live in, your own home, your garden, the office, your living space, your car, your bedroom, and even your closet. Your environment is influenced by those you live with, so consider them a part of it. How much joy do your surroundings bring you?

1   2   3   4   5   6   7   8   9   10

RECREATION & RELAXATION

This includes the fun stuff: your vacation time, free time, hobbies, fun pursuits outside of work, like movies, sports, reading, journaling, painting, leisurely walks, and activities you use to recharge. Consider the frequency and quality of your recreation/ relaxation time. How satisfied with it are you?

1   2   3   4   5   6   7   8   9   10

PERSONALITY GROWTH

This area encompasses your efforts to be a better you. It includes developmental activities like attending conferences, seminars, workshops, self-improvement reading, and educational pursuits. It also covers less formal attempts at growth, such as introspective reflection, bettering your interpersonal skills, reading this book ;) and anything you do to improve habits and skills. You may do these things subconsciously, to advance self-awareness and identity or enhance the quality of your life. Or they may be intentional, meant to develop specific talents, to increase your employability, or to realize dreams and aspirations. How is this all working out for you?

1 2 3 4 5 6 7 8 9 10

SPIRITUALITY & FAITH

This area includes your belief in a higher power, God, or a metaphysical force that is greater than the physical world. This area can include your devotion to your religion, divinity, faith, or the practice of honoring powers that transcend the physical world. Also consider prayer, devotion, meditation and/or the practice of being "present," living in the moment. How much personal satisfaction do you gain from your practices—or lack of them?

1 2 3 4 5 6 7 8 9 10

PURPOSE & CAREER

This includes your profession, volunteer work, following your passion, and doing what you believe you've been called to do. It also includes knowing and understanding your why. Do you use your talents or any work/knowledge/training/skill/or natural ability in a way that has a positive effect on others? Do you believe that who you are, what you do, and how you use your "calling" or gifts positively affects others?

1 2 3 4 5 6 7 8 9 10

FINANCIAL

This includes your relationship with money: your current savings, lack of debt, sound investments, and financial independence. Related issues, like your understanding of your financial situation, your ability to afford the things you want, and the outlook for your financial future also contribute to your state of mind. How satisfied are you with these things?

1 2 3 4 5 6 7 8 9 10

FRIENDS & FAMILY RELATIONSHIPS

This area includes your parents, siblings, and close relationships you might have with extended family members. It also includes your relationship with a small circle of close friends. Put together, how fulfilling do you find the level of mutual support, respect, "real" communication, and your personal and emotional connections with friends and family?

ROMANTIC RELATIONSHIPS

1   2   3   4   5   6   7   8   9   10

This area can include your significant other, your dating relationships, and/or your spouse. This is a measure of your emotional and physical connection with a romantic partner. In evaluating this area, take into consideration your mutual support, respect, appreciation and friendship. Take into account shared hobbies, amount and quality of time spent together, and your physical and intimate connection. How well do you feel supported and connected to your partner(s)?

FITNESS& PHYSICAL HEALTH

1   2   3   4   5   6   7   8   9   10

This is a broad category but generally includes your overall "wellness." Think about the factors of your physical health: regular diet, stress management, sleep, exercise, and nutrition. What degree of flexibility, strength, and energy do they result in? Are you satisfied with your weight? Does your level of fitness—and the things you do to achieve it—make you happy?

EMOTIONAL HEALTH

1   2   3   4   5   6   7   8   9   10

This category includes how you feel about yourself and your importance to others. How easily do you feel and express (when appropriate) a wide range of emotions without feeling unsafe or insecure? Mental wellness includes your overall happiness, a feeling of being whole, satisfied and at peace with your past. Mental wellness is your ability to handle stress and life's unexpected turns. How often do you feel sad, angry, depressed, shame, or emptiness? How okay are you with yourself?

GIVING

1   2   3   4   5   6   7   8   9   10

This area is about how you are contributing to the world around you. Are you giving back in various ways that you are able to, with your time, talents, knowledge, and finances? Is there more you could be doing to give to your family, tribe, community or the greater good? Think about your God given gifts and how you can use them to serve. How do you feel about what you are offering in each of these areas?

EXPLORE

1   2   3   4   5   6   7   8   9   10

This category is about how often you are willing to get out of your comfort zone. This could be in trying new things, exploring new areas, delving into new endeavors, and your sense of adventure. Are you feeling complacent or fulfilled in this area?

"Oh, darling, your **priorities** will change."
—Krystel Stacey

#SheMindsHerOwnBusiness

STEP 2: A SHIFT IN FOCUS

1. List any area you rated a 6 or below in here:

2. List any area that received a score of 7 or higher in another group.

3. Now find a way to celebrate in each of the areas in which you scored a 7 or above. Well done! Reward yourself for your hard work in whatever way you see fit, and keep doing what you're doing well.

List your reward for your top areas here:

4. Take some time to think about why you rated yourself low in the areas that totaled 6 or below. Usually, these are areas of your life that you really care about, or that you want to improve but with which you are struggling. Why do you think these scored so low?

5. What's holding you back from improvement in those areas?

6. List 3 things you could do to improve those areas here:

1.

2.

3.

> ## This was no longer the Dumbo ride, my friends.

KRYSTEL STACEY

#SheMindsHerOwnBusiness

Core
Priorities.

V

S
Key
Priorities.

Stagnant
businesses rot.

Evolving

in your business is a must.
What has worked in the past
might not work now.

———

Krystel Stacey

1. What is a core priority for you? It's innately ingrained in you, so you probably scored high in this area.

2. Which of your lowest-scoring areas would make the greatest difference if you were to change them in the next three months? Choose your lowest three first; then select one out of those areas that would make the biggest difference in your life if you were to improve in this area.

3. This ONE area that would make the greatest difference is your **KEY PRIORITY**. This is what you are going to focus on for the next three to six months. This is the key to making a difference in your life.

4. How are you going to hold yourself accountable to this key priority? What could you do or whom can you ask to keep you on track toward making this your MAIN priority in life?

"the sweet sixteen."
-Krystel Stacey

1 BRANDING.

2 PROFITABILITY.

3 PROCESSES & SYSTEMS.

4 TEAM BUILDING.

5 MARKETING.

6 PRICES AND PACKAGING.

7 ENVIRONMENT.

8 EQUIPMENT.

9 CUSTOMER RELATIONSHIP MANAGEMENT (CRM).

10 CUSTOMER ACQUISITION.

11 CUSTOMER SERVICE.

12 NETWORKING.

13 WEBSITE.

14 SOCIAL MEDIA.

15 FINANCES/BOOKKEEPING.

16 LEADERSHIP/ACCOUNTABILITY.

#SheMindsHerOwnBusiness

Now, keeping your life's key priority in mind, let's talk about your business:

I have come up with the **sweet sixteen** areas of your business.
Rank yourself—not on external conditions, but on things that you do or could have control over.

1 = I am really lacking this in my business.

10 = I am INCREDIBLE at this!

Area of Business

BRANDING _____
This includes the entire aesthetic of your brand: logo, colors, style, typography, etc.

PROFITABILITY _____
How much profit are you keeping? How profitable is your business financially? Are your expenses as lean as they can/should be? Are you paying yourself regularly? Do you have cash on hand or are you operating check to check?

PROCESSES & SYSTEMS _____
Have you created standard operating procedures for your company? Do you have step by step processes and systems in place that are clearly defined?

TEAM BUILDING _____
How are you growing your internal team—not just in size, but in loyalty and education? How are you hiring? How are you firing? Are you delegating properly?

MARKETING _____

This includes press, public relations, editorials, and the visibility of your business to the public.

PRICES AND PACKAGING _____

This includes your current packages (services offered or actual physical packaging) and pricing of your services or product.

ENVIRONMENT _____

Where do you work? This could be your home office, a public office, or a warehouse. Is the environment around you enabling you to do your job better, be creative, or focus when needed?

EQUIPMENT _____

Do you have the equipment you need to run your business properly? Is it updated to current standards?

CUSTOMER RELATIONSHIP MANAGEMENT (CRM) _____

How are you keeping track of the clients you have or have had? How are you managing what needs to be done for them or what has been done for them in the past?

CUSTOMER ACQUISITION _____

How are you getting your customers ? Do you feel good about the systems you have in place for obtaining new customers?

CUSTOMER SERVICE _____

What is the customer's experience with your company? Once you have the customers, how effectively are you communicating with them? And how are they experiencing your brand?

NETWORKING   ————————

This includes how you are interacting with others to develop contacts and keep up current business relationships. This could include going to events, making a point to meet with new people, and maintaining the contacts you currently have.

WEBSITE   ————————

How do you feel about your current website? Does it match the brand you have created? How is the customer experience on the website? Is your messaging on the site clear?

SOCIAL MEDIA ————————

This includes your Instagram, Facebook, LinkedIn accounts, and any other social media presence you have. Are you communicating effectively which services you have to offer and creating a cohesive brand with all of your social media? Also, think about your activity on social media.

FINANCES/BOOKKEEPING   ————————

How are you keeping track of your finances? Do you have an effective system for bookkeeping, and are you producing profit and loss statements regularly? Are you reconciling your accounts monthly?

LEADERSHIP/ACCOUNTABILITY   ————————

Are you able to lead effectively in your business? Do you have an accountability metric to make sure you are maintaining standards?

(EACH OF THESE AREAS NEED RANKINGS.)

List your **3 top** areas:

1

2

3

How will you celebrate these parts of your business?

List your **3 lowest** areas:

1

2

3

List 3 ways you can you think of to improve in these areas:

Social Challenge

ON YOUR GRID AND IN YOUR STORIES ON INSTAGRAM AND FACEBOOK

Priorities- It's time to share your **Key Priority**. Share with your followers what you are choosing to focus on at this time, bringing them on the journey with you. Have them help you stay focused on your key priority in a positive way.

*Add the hashtag #SheMindsHerOwnBusiness and tag @krystelstacey for reposting.

Sure, unexpected things happened, and it wasn't just a straight line to success. But I planned for where I wanted to go. And that's how I got to where I am.

—

KRYSTEL STACEY

1. What is the main area in which you could create growth that would open doors to many other possibilities?

2. Key Business Priority:

3. WHAT are you going to do to work on this area?

4. HOW are you going to be held accountable to this?

Social Challenge

ON YOUR GRID AND IN YOUR STORIES ON INSTAGRAM AND FACEBOOK

Priorities- It's time to share your **Business Key Priority**. Share with your followers what you are choosing to focus on at this time in your business, bring them on the journey with you. Have them help you stay focused on your key priority.
** Some of your followers may have resources to help you. Ask them to share.

*Add the hashtag #SheMindsHerOwnBusiness and tag @krystelstacey for reposting.

CHAPTER

four

GOAL SETTING

"she
believed she could,
so she
did."

gem goals

the purpose of GEM is to set goals for yourself that are both obtainable and trackable. we encourage you to take action and set goals within these criteria.

The goals we are going to set must have the following attributes:

G GRITTY

they are very specific and detailed.

E EFFECTIVE

the results will make a difference in your life; they're attainable and relevant.

M MEASURABLE

you're able to measure them and hold yourself accountable with a time frame and a due date. These also have to be achievable in the next 90 days.

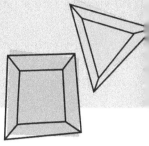

List 1 goal that focuses on your new KEY PRIORITY.

    1.

List 2 goals that have to do with the next 2 areas of your **life** in which you ranked lowest.

    1.

    2.

List 3 goals that have to do with the 3 areas of your **business** in which you ranked lowest.

    1.

    2.

    3.

Now list 3 more goals (free for all, can be anything in **business or life** that you believe will make the greatest difference for you this year).

    1.

    2.

3.
Write your goals out as if they have already happened or you have already accomplished them. So when you reach the goal, you are _____. You have _____. And you do _____.

I AM	I HAVE	I DO

1

GOAL

ACTION STEPS

1.

2.

3.

4.

RESOURCES

who or what could help?

DUE DATE

CELEBRATE

with...

2

GOAL

ACTION STEPS

1.

2.

3.

4.

RESOURCES

who or what could help?

DUE DATE

CELEBRATE

with...

3

GOAL

ACTION STEPS

1.

2.

3.

4.

RESOURCES
who or what could help?

DUE DATE

CELEBRATE
with...

4

GOAL

ACTION STEPS

1.

2.

3.

4.

RESOURCES
who or what could help?

DUE DATE

CELEBRATE
with...

5

GOAL

ACTION STEPS

1.

2.

3.

4.

RESOURCES

who or what could help?

DUE DATE

CELEBRATE

with...

6

GOAL

ACTION STEPS

1.

2.

3.

4.

RESOURCES

who or what could help?

DUE DATE

CELEBRATE

with...

7

GOAL

ACTION STEPS

1.

2.

3.

4.

RESOURCES
who or what could help?

DUE DATE

CELEBRATE
with...

8

GOAL

ACTION STEPS

1.

2.

3.

4.

RESOURCES
who or what could help?

DUE DATE

CELEBRATE
with...

GOAL

ACTION STEPS

1.

2.

3.

4.

RESOURCES
who or what could help?

DUE DATE

CELEBRATE
with...

Are you happy with the goals above?
If so, **move on.**
If not, go back and create new goals.

"Oh, but everybody thinks
That everybody knows
About everybody else
Nobody knows
Anything about themselves
Cause they're all worried about
everybody else."

JACK JOHNSON

#SheMindsHerOwnBusiness

Now that you have your nine goals, write out one to three resources you will need to accomplish these goals. Some examples of resources are: time, finances, accountability, physical tools or supplies, and someone who can help you.

1.

2.

3.

4.

5.

6.

7.

8.

9.

Did you notice that you repeated any of the resources you need? If none are repetitive, then list which resource you need the most:

"

BRILLIANT goal:
it's the goal you create to bring you the resources you need the most.

———

KRYSTEL STACEY

#SheMindsHerOwnBusiness

NOW it's time to write out your BRILLIANT goal (goal #10). This goal sheds light on the rest of the GEM goals. It will be the one major task that will help you accomplish many of your other objectives, because it will help you get the resources you need.

My Brilliant Goal is:

10

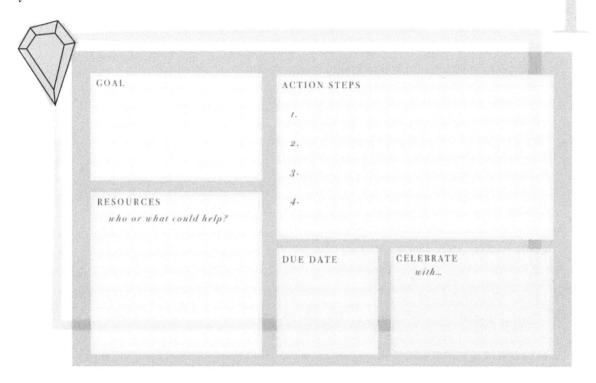

GOAL

RESOURCES
who or what could help?

ACTION STEPS

1.

2.

3.

4.

DUE DATE

CELEBRATE
with...

Brainstorm a list of actions that will help you reach this brilliant goal.

Go back through and number your ideas, starting with the best idea as number 1. Then, you are going to try it and see if it works! If not, move on to idea number 2, and so on. If you get to a point where nothing is working, then you may need to brainstorm again. That's okay. Trust me; it will come.

1. With this list of 10 goals, go through and break down each goal into multiple steps. Each step should take you 20 minutes or less.

2. Schedule these steps on your calendar so you complete 2 of them each day. That's 20 to 40 minutes per day, 5 days a week.

You've just sealed a deal with

yourself.

This list is your pattern for the
next ninety days.

You have just designed your life!
Celebrate that, all by itself.

—

Krystel Stacey

Once you have mapped it out, give each of your 10 goals a due date (within 90 days!).

Last, but not least, write down how you will celebrate when you accomplish each goal. What are you going to do that will be really special for you when you reach a goal? For the 9 supporting GEM goals, maybe that's something small or having to do with self-care. But your BRILLIANT GOAL needs to be something big—really celebrate and bask in your accomplishment!

GOAL	DUE DATE	REWARD

A good goal truly is a

gem,

something so precious
and special you should

treasure it!

———

Krystel Stacey

Social Challenge

Share your GEM goals with your followers, ask them to help you reach them by_____ . Or ask them to share some of their own goals for the year and ask how you can help them. Or do both by sharing this in two separate posts. This is a great way to connect with your followers, be vulnerable with them telling them what you are working on and give them the opportunity to share with you.

Time to get authentic on social!

***You can do the above in a post or in a story, however, I recommend doing both.
1. Post it on your grid. 2. Later break it down more in stories and ask them to share (using question box, or poll, or have them DM you).
It's up to you and how you would normally talk to your followers but remember it's important to keep them engaged with you.

*Add the hashtag #SheMindsHerOwnBusiness and tag @krystelstacey for reposting.

For every decision you make from here

on out, consider how it will play into

where you want to be in five years.

Don't waste time on what

won't move you forward.

Plan how you will celebrate

when you accomplish them.

Five

THE FINE ART OF SCHEDULING

"I don't want to get to the end of my life and find that I just lived the length of it. I want to have lived the width of it as well."
—Diane Ackerman

#SheMindsHerOwnBusiness

Don't chase someone else's idea of a dream schedule. Seriously, dig deep and figure out what you would want. Suppose you had no obligations. Would you work? Would you play? Would you do something else meaningful? Next, factor in your prior obligations but still find time to do some of the things you crave.

1. What time would you wake up?

2. What time would you meditate, pray, and/or journal?

3. When will you exercise?

4. How many hours a day do you want to work? Do you enjoy work? Is it fun?

5. How many hours of leisure do you want in a day?

6. Which time of day would you devote to what it is you love doing? To your work? Your purpose? Your passion? Your business? Your hobby?

7. What time would you schedule to catch up with friends?

8. What time would you devote to family?

9. What time of day would you turn everything off and relax?

10. What time of day would you spend organizing?

11. What would the perfect schedule look like?

12. What time should you go to bed?

13. What could you do for hours and not get tired? What is your favorite part of your job?

14. What do you love doing that recharges you? This should be something that doesn't relate to work, but that you wish you could do every day.

15. What is the one thing that, if you spent more time doing in your business, would make a lasting difference? This should be something that makes progress TAKE OFF.

Time is our most valuable asset,
and it's one we squander the most.

I spent those hours reacting,
instead of being proactive.

———

KRYSTEL STACEY

16. What is the most valuable place for you to spend your time?

17. Think about the last time you were nervous, anxious, or worried. Was it due to finances? Getting a customer? What has upset you or made you nervous? What do you not like? List it.

18. What percentage of the time do you feel stressed out and overwhelmed? Defeated? HONESTLY?

1. What is your chronotype?

2. What does this mean for the time you are most productive?

3. What does this mean for the time you are least productive?

"Don't say you don't have enough time.
You have **exactly the same** number of hours per day that were given to Helen Keller, Pasteur, Michelangelo, Mother Teresa, Leonardo da Vinci, Thomas Jefferson, and Albert Einstein."
—H. Jackson Brown, Jr.

#SheMindsHerOwnBusiness

1. If you were to win the lottery tomorrow, what would you spend your day doing? How much of what you are doing right now would you continue doing?

2. What brings you joy? What makes you happy?

3. What is one thing you hope you never have to do again?

4. Who do you wish you had a better relationship with?

5. How often would you like to go on vacation?

6. If you were able to retire and could just "dabble" in your business, where would you would spend most of your time?

7. What do you feel you are missing out on?

8. What do you wish someone else would notice about you?

9. What area of your life feels out of balance?

10. What would help your personal life and work feel more in balance?

11. What makes you feel like you are living your purpose? What do you want to be doing? What is or could be your purpose or your calling?

12. What do you do that makes an impact on others?

There are secrets to **perfect timing.** Take advantage of your own peak work time.

—Krystel Stacey

#SheMindsHerOwnBusiness

Now get out your calendar. If you have a physical planner or calendar, put pen to paper. If you prefer to go paperless, use your computer phone app, or an online calendar to schedule things out. Begin with your essentials, and then build out blocks of time - for work, leisure, and family.

Now narrow it down more.

*Keep in mind your chronotype.

Social Challenge

Scheduling: Have you created a new schedule for yourself yet?
Talk about it, if you haven't already.
Then choose one thing that you do want to change in your schedule
and ask your followers to hold you accountable to it.

***You can do the above in a post or in a story, however, I recommend doing both.
1. Post it on your grid. 2. Later break it down more in stories and ask them to share
(using question box, or poll, or have them DM you).
It's up to you and how you would normally talk to your followers but remember it's
important to keep them engaged with you.

*Add the hashtag #SheMindsHerOwnBusiness and tag @krystelstacey for reposting.

"Today
I am going to really reevaluate my life. I am going to do this differently. I am going to make a plan that works best for me."

KRYSTEL STACEY

#SheMindsHerOwnBusiness

You have to make a shift. We had to write the above things down to see what you LOVE, and what you really hate; what you want to maybe change in your life, or do more of, or less of. Now you can start to make a plan and design your beautiful life.

	MON	TUES	WED	THURS	FRI	SAT	SUN
5 AM							
6 AM							
7 AM							
8 AM							
9 AM							
10 AM							
11 AM							
12 PM							
1 PM							
2 PM							
3 PM							
4 PM							

5 PM						
6 PM						
7 PM						
8 PM						
9 PM						
10 PM						
11 PM						
12 PM						
1 AM						
2 AM						
3 AM						
4 AM						

Wouldn't it be crazy if you got to
do all of the things you wanted to do...

Begin with your essentials,
then build out blocks of time

Making a schedule doesn't have to be
daunting or put unreasonable demands on our time.

Ultimately, by doing this, we are freeing
ourselves to create more—to create
beautiful moments, golden opportunities,
efficiency, experiences, and memories.

———

KRYSTEL STACEY

#SheMindsHerOwnBusiness

Map out the big picture for the next 5 years.

YEAR	FOCUS FOR THE YEAR	4 MAJOR PROJECTS	3-MONTH BREAKDOWN
1		1	JAN - MARCH:
		2	APRIL - JUNE:
		3	JULY - SEPT:
		4	OCT - DEC:

YEAR	FOCUS FOR THE YEAR	4 MAJOR PROJECTS	3-MONTH BREAKDOWN
2		1	JAN - MARCH:
		2	APRIL - JUNE:
		3	JULY - SEPT:
		4	OCT - DEC:

119

YEAR	FOCUS FOR THE YEAR	4 MAJOR PROJECTS	3-MONTH BREAKDOWN
3		1	JAN - MARCH:
		2	APRIL - JUNE:
		3	JULY - SEPT:
		4	OCT - DEC:

YEAR	FOCUS FOR THE YEAR	4 MAJOR PROJECTS	3-MONTH BREAKDOWN
4		1	JAN - MARCH:
		2	APRIL - JUNE:
		3	JULY - SEPT:
		4	OCT - DEC:
5	FOCUS FOR THE YEAR	4 MAJOR PROJECTS	3-MONTH BREAKDOWN
		1	JAN - MARCH:
		2	APRIL - JUNE:
		3	JULY - SEPT:
		4	OCT - DEC:

"

There is so much you can do
when you make scheduling an art.

You need to be the artist of your own life.
You get to design it.

Every moment of every day is
ultimately up to you.
What will you do with it?

KRYSTEL STACEY

#SheMindsHerOwnBusiness

"What you do today is important because you are exchanging a day of your **life for it."**

—Elizabeth George

#SheMindsHerOwnBusiness

find your focus.

To create something exceptional,
your mindset must be
relentlessly focused on the
smallest detail.
—Giorgio Armani

#SheMindsHerOwnBusiness

F | Find time each day to work on your goals.

When will you work on your goals? What specific amount of time are you setting aside daily to work on your goals?

O | Old ways won't open new doors.

You are going to have to be creative in how you do things now. Don't go through the same doors you have in the past.

What doors have you tried before that have not worked?

What new doors could you try?

C | Create new habits.

This could be setting your alarm in your phone to tell you when to move on to the next task or a time-saving action that frees you up for more focused activity.

What new habits are you going to form to help you FOCUS?

U | Utilize your resources.

What resources could you use that you haven't yet?

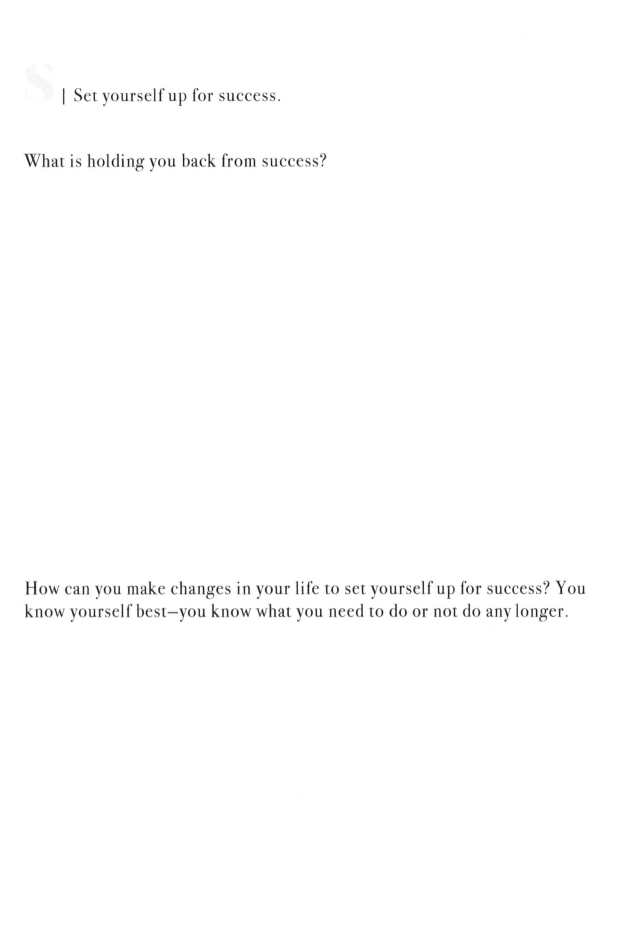

| Set yourself up for success.

What is holding you back from success?

How can you make changes in your life to set yourself up for success? You know yourself best—you know what you need to do or not do any longer.

"

No matter
your age or experience, focus is key.

No matter
what you have been through or where
you are going, if you concentrate on
what you want—armed with specific
goals and a great plan—you can
achieve it.

KRYSTEL STACEY

#SheMindsHerOwnBusiness

Social Challenge

F.O.C.U.S.- Share where you are focusing your direction for the future.

***You can do the above in a post or in a story, however, I recommend doing both.
1. Post it on your grid. 2. Later break it down more in stories and ask them to share (using question box, or poll, or have them DM you).

Don't be distracted, FOCUS on where you are going.

*Add the hashtag #SheMindsHerOwnBusiness and tag @krystelstacey for reposting.

It's time to find a way to keep your notes all in one place. This is going to be huge for you. Instead of a million sticky notes, phone notes, planner scribbles, notebook jottings, etc., you are going to choose just ONE place to keep all of your lists and notes that is most convenient for you. It needs to be somewhere that is easy for you and tangible.

Where will you keep your notes?

In writing down your new note location, you make a commitment to yourself to take notes in this 1 place. It will save you so much time in the long run to have your to-do lists, goals, etc., all in one place. Now, go do it!

how
do I make it stop?

How do I create order
and engage in
organization?

———

Krystel Stacey

Here are four steps to help you FOCUS on your goals:

1.

Set aside a date each month to create your monthly goals:

What date will this be each month (such as the first Tuesday or the first day of each month)?

What works best for you and your schedule? You will need to set aside time on your calendar to do this.

2.

Reserve a day each week when you will set your daily goals:

Usually what works best is Sunday or Monday. Set aside an hour just to work on what your goals will look like each day for that week.

3. Set aside time daily before the "whirlwind" to create a to-do list:

When works best for you?

Do you need to start a new habit of waking up an hour earlier, to spend time working on this and to have a little time to yourself before your day begins? Or do you need to change the way you work? For instance, instead of picking up your phone the moment you wake up, you'll pick up your notebook and begin to write down a to-do list.

4. Figure out a prioritizing system that works best for you. Remember to try and get the harder tasks done first, such as the ones you don't want to do or are struggling with. How will you prioritize, from most to least urgent?

F | Find time each day to work on your goals.

To do this, set aside time devoted solely to working toward your goals.

O | Old ways won't open new doors.

You will need to be creative in how you do things now. Don't just
go through the same doors you have in the past.

C | Create new habits.

Make reminders and motivation easy and automatic. Set your phone
alarm to tell you when to move on to the next task. Post your aspirations where
you can see them every day.

U | Utilize your resources.

I'm sure you have resources at your fingertips you aren't using
yet. It's time to inventory those, so you can reach for them when you need them.

S | Set yourself up for success.

Take away your distractions. Devise systems to avoid getting caught
up in competing concerns. Set yourself up for success, stay organized, and focus
on your key priority and the goals you have set for yourself.

———

KRYSTEL STACEY

#SheMindsHerOwnBusiness

FOCUS on yourself and your BRAND. Reach down deep into your more authentic, true self and find your aesthetic. Answering these questions will help you bring *you* into your brand.

1. What are your personal values?

2. What is your personal aesthetic; what would you say your style is?

3. What are your brand values?

4. What is your brand aesthetic?

5. How does your business aesthetic differ from your personal style, if at all?

6. Think about seven-year-old you. What would she say about you and your brand?

7. How can you become more like her again?

Staying organized is paramount. Like the tailoring of a couture gown, it must be done bit by bit—in order. It's meticulous work, but if you're organized, it will pay off in unimaginable ways.

Krystel Stacey

#SheMindsHerOwnBusiness

Why wait another second?
Open yourself
up to be able to move onto
the other,
bigger things.

———————————————

KRYSTEL STACEY

#SheMindsHerOwnBusiness

CHAPTER
seven

BUILDING YOUR TRIBE.

Visionary Planning

1. Monthly Goals

2. Daily Goals

3. To-Do Lists

4. PRIORITIZE

Krystel Stacey

#SheMindsHerOwnBusiness

While I want you to OWN every aspect of your business, I know that it's impossible to DO every aspect of your business. You must delegate.

1. What do you want to do in your business?

2. What aspects of your business do you absolutely love doing day to day?

3. What aspects of your day-to-day do you dread?

4. What aspects can only you do?

5. What things that you do every day could someone else do?

6. What things must you be involved with daily?

7. What things can you let go of but still oversee?

"

Giving someone else the opportunity
to create a role for themselves
and grow with the company was one
of the most valuable things I could
have done in the delegation
department.

KRYSTEL STACEY

#SheMindsHerOwnBusiness

8. Where do you need the most help?

9. What are your greatest strengths?

10. What are your weaknesses?

11. If you had the money to hire someone right now, whom would you hire?

12. After looking over all of the above, what do you think would most help you?

13. List the attributes of whom you want to hire before you begin interviewing; this will help you weed out candidates quickly.

14. Where can you start looking for someone to hire? (online or locally)

15. What do you need to organize in your business before you can turn that aspect over to someone else?

16. What systems can you create to help the people you hire in the future?

17. What steps or standard operating procedures (SOPs) can you create to make your processes easier?

18. Which processes could you create SOPs for?

19. What are the steps to creating these?

Newsflash: you must **delegate.**

—Krystel Stacey

#SheMindsHerOwnBusiness

Social Challenge

Head to the hashtag- #SheMindsHerOwnBusiness on Instagram and comment on ten posts (having to do with the book). It's time to start helping each other out, comment, like/love on each other's posts. Have fun with this! This is how you begin to build your TRIBE, which we are also focusing on this week in the reading.

*You can do this once a week or once a month to really grow your reach and **connect with like-minded women.**

Now you know why we have you #SheMindsHerOwnBusiness, it really will help you **BUILD YOUR TRIBE!**

1. How will you lead?

2. If you lead by example, what would that look like?

3. How can you show your team how to do something instead of telling them?

"The greatest gift you can give to someone is to

believe

in them."

———————

– Unknown

Social Challenge

ON YOUR GRID AND IN YOUR STORIES ON INSTAGRAM AND FACEBOOK

Build your Tribe- It's time to build your tribe of followers! How you ask?

1. This week you are going to create a post (with valuable information) or a giveaway where people can tag their friends... grow your tribe by GIVING.

2. Ask for the help you need... if you know you need to delegate and you know exactly what it is you need- it's time to ask for it- ask if others have any recommendations or any ideas... it's all about collaboration and word-of-mouth recommendations are always great too!

*Add the hashtag #SheMindsHerOwnBusiness and tag @krystelstacey for reposting.

1. Define your ideal clients.

2. Where do they live?

3. How old are they?

4. Where do they work (if they work)?

5. Where do they spend their free time?

> "

Stop looking at everyone else's stories and begin selling your own.

_____

KRYSTEL STACEY

#SheMindsHerOwnBusiness

6. What car do they drive?

7. What's their favorite color?

8. Where do they shop?

9. Do they have kids (how many)?

10. Do they have pets?

11. What kind of lifestyle do they have?

12. Do they work out?

13. What do they eat?

14. What's their favorite movie(s)?

15. What's their favorite book(s)?

16. What else do you know about them?

Name them:

> ## "
>
> # Nothing is impossible. It might take extra time and effort, but our work must be done right, or why do it at all?

KRYSTEL STACEY

#SheMindsHerOwnBusiness

CHAPTER

review.
refine.
edit.
get after it!

"Never give up on a dream just because of the time it will take to accomplish it. The time will pass anyway."

EARL NIGHTINGALE

#SheMindsHerOwnBusiness

1. Looking at the last 6 months of business, if you were your own client, how would you review your service or product?

2. What services or products do you need to let go of?

3. What new products or services could you offer to replace them?

4. What products or services could you sell more of and focus more energy on if you got rid of your worst-performing ones?

Sometimes you have to let things go that are no longer working or serving you.

Krystel Stacey

#SheMindsHerOwnBusiness

1. Have you received a bad review(s) from someone else about your service or product?

2. If you are honest with yourself, is any of it true?

3. If so, what do you need to change or refine? If not, how can put yourself in the clients' shoes, see it from their perspective, and make sure that this level of dissatisfaction doesn't happen again?

> "Don't you worry your pretty little mind, people throw rocks at things that shine."

TAYLOR SWIFT

#SheMindsHerOwnBusiness

1. What are you going to edit right now in your business?

2. Do you need to edit your aesthetic?

3. Do you need to edit your services and product offerings?

4. Do you need to edit your message, or the way you are communicating what you do and why you do it?

The truth is, in
business as in life,
you get to choose
what you
focus on.

––––––––

Krystel Stacey

66

"Edit" runs on repeat in my head because there are so many things I love, activities I want to do, business ideas and décor items I want to create. I constantly have to stop and remind myself to edit.

KRYSTEL STACEY

#SheMindsHerOwnBusiness

1. What area of your life do you need to JUMP into? Take that leap!

2. How can you grow in confidence?

3. What would give you more confidence?

4. How can you show your confidence or become an expert in your area?

Start with what you know about yourself. What do you believe about yourself? Which characteristics do you possess? What do you need? What do you know is true about yourself but that you sometimes need to be reminded of? Write it down:

I am:

I have:

I live in:

I am committed to:

I will:

I can:

I will not:

If you are feeling unsure, list all of the people that love you or that you know you can trust—even if it's just one person, your pet, or God. That's okay. This helps to remind yourself of the positives in life.

What reminders or triggers do you need to set on your phone or throughout your home or office?

If I am going to bet on
anyone, it's going to be

myself.

Krystel Stacey

Social Challenge

ON YOUR GRID AND IN YOUR STORIES ON INSTAGRAM AND FACEBOOK

Share what you are most excited about in the future… put your dreams out there- when you write it down it's so much more likely to happen. When you put it out there on Instagram for ALL TO SEE, it's very likely to come true!

You can do the above in a post or in a story or I recommend doing both. 1. Post it on a post and then later break it down more in stories and ask them to interact with you.

*Add the hashtag #SheMindsHerOwnBusiness and tag @krystelstacey for reposting.

No. 9
HIGH STANDARDS

"Keep your heels, head, and standards high!"

———

COCO CHANEL

#SheMindsHerOwnBusiness

1. What is non-negotiable in your business?

2. What are the MAIN standards for your business? (list 3 to 5 standards)

3. Brainstorm your ALWAYS and NEVER statements. Once they are perfected write them on the next few pages.

What will you always do? From here on out you are going to **"say hello"** to these being part of your life and business!

I will always ...

oh, hello

love always. me

oh, hello

love always. me

oh, hello

love always. me

oh, hello

love always. me

"Fool me once,
shame on you;
fool me twice,
shame on me."

GEORGE HORNE

#SheMindsHerOwnBusiness

I WILL NEVER...
(things I am kissing goodbye!)

Why not set the

standards high?

Krystel Stacey

#SheMindsHerOwnBusiness

Social Challenge

ON YOUR GRID AND IN YOUR STORIES ON INSTAGRAM AND FACEBOOK

Post your standards for your network.
You can do this in one post but we would recommend spreading it out over the course of a week or a month, focusing each post on one standard. Creating posts and stories that let your followers get to know you and better understand why you do things the way you do.
You are introducing them to the standards that you believe in.

BONUS BRAINSTORM SESSION | FAILURE

Feel free to come back to this one if/when you fail, to help you get through it.

1. Have you had any failures in your business?

2. What did you or could you have learned from your failures?

3. If you were fearless, what would you do next?

> So, in life and in business, we really need to evaluate and set standards that are **beneficial** —not just traditional

Krystel Stacey

Chapter ten

RULES
TO
LIVE
BY

"If you have good thoughts, they will shine out of your face like sunbeams, and you will always look lovely"

ROALD DAHL

#SheMindsHerOwnBusiness

Based on the projected future of business, there are 4 areas in which we humans can compete. Which one(s) are you going to base your business on? Circle it, and then write about how you can incorporate these into your 5-year plan and beyond.

1. Creativity

2. Imagination

3. Intuition

4. Curiosity

How?

I have decided to paint my own *positive* reality.
I live with my head in the clouds and my feet on the ground.
I *celebrate* the tiny victories.
I get excited over the details.
I *believe* in God (even though I don't fully understand why
things happen the way they do).
I *believe* in love and fairy tales.
I call a spade a spade, and I mean what I say.
I *choose* to see people as beautiful, lovely, kind, and fabulous
—and if they disappointment me, so be it.
At least I *believed* in them.

———

KRYSTEL STACEY

#SheMindsHerOwnBusiness

Visit https://enneagramtest.net/ and take the test to learn your personality strengths and weaknesses.

1. What is your enneagram number? (circle your number)

$$1 \quad 3 \quad 5 \quad 7 \quad 9$$

$$2 \quad 4 \quad 6 \quad 8$$

2. What have you learned about yourself by understanding your number?

3. What are your strengths?

4. What are your weaknesses?

5. Is there anything that the enneagram says about your personality type that you do not believe is true?

6. What do you believe is MOST true about you?

"You know all of those things you have always wanted to do? **You should do them."**

———

Unknown

Think about the 4 commitments you can make, suggested by Don Miguel Ruiz in his book, The Four Agreements:

1. Be impeccable with your word.

2. Don't take anything personally.

3. Don't make assumptions.

4. Always do your best.

1. Which of the 4 agreements do you most need to work on?

2. Why?

3. What are your own rules that you will live by? (You are welcome to use my rules, but I would also love for you to create some of your own.)

4. It's time to LIVE IT OUT and to OWN IT. What are your next steps?

"

Your real purpose is
minding your own business,
figuring out who you are, and using
your unique gifts to lead yourself to
success.

KRYSTEL STACEY

#SheMindsHerOwnBusiness

Social Challenge

SHARE what you have learned about yourself and your business!

Share your truest self with your followers by divulging your big dreams, purpose, values, GEM goals and Brilliant Goal. They want to know! They want to be a part of your journey. Invite them, have them join you in this adventure, and CELEBRATE with them when you accomplish your goals. We suggest sharing with your followers every step of the way.

Now that you have completed the book and workbook we would love to invite you to apply to our Book Ambassador Program, please visit **SheMindsHerOwnBusiness.com** to do so.

The Four Agreements

1. Be impeccable with your word.
2. Don't take anything personally.
3. Don't make assumptions.
4. Always do your best.

———

DON MIGUEL RUIZ

#SheMindsHerOwnBusiness

Congratulations!

Making it through this workbook is a huge accomplishment. You know where you are, where you want to be, the steps it will take to get there.

Now, go celebrate, and continue to:

mind your own business!

#SheMindsHerOwnBusiness

XO,

"

"To live is the rarest thing in the world. Most people exist, that is all."

_____

OSCAR WILDE

#SheMindsHerOwnBusiness

CPSIA information can be obtained
at www.ICGtesting.com
Printed in the USA
BVHW021402150421
605036BV00009B/1402